Coffee For Everyday Use

Jacob Ray

Copyright © 2019 Jacob Ray
All rights reserved.
ISBN-13: 9781081121709

The author, to the best of his ability, has tested and evaluated all statements, concepts, and suggestions presented in this publication to ensure that there are no factual errors.

This book is dedicated…

To Dad: the one who told me how to brew his Maxwell House the right way when I was eight years old.

To Alley: the one who tries the coffee I make without question.

Table Of Contents

Introduction

7

How To Use This Book

11

Part One: Before You Drink
What Exactly Is Coffee?

15

What Happens In Roasting?

27

Part Two: How To Drink Now
How Do I Order At A Coffee Shop?

39

How Do I Pick Beans To Bring Home With Me?

49

How Should I Brew This Coffee?

59

Part Three: How To Drink Later
How Should I Keep This Coffee From Going Bad?

81

Epilogue

91

About The Author

Introduction

Coffee is an amazing and ever-twisting journey that will break your heart right after it fills you with joy. I've spent the last three years working diligently to figure out how to make this journey more enjoyable to those who have only had heartbreak when it comes to this beautiful brown liquid. By no means have I arrived or unlocked any hidden secret that tenured baristas and dedicated researchers have yet to find, but I would consider myself somewhat of a professional in educating both the coffee enthusiast and novice on coffee knowledge on both sides of the service bar.

The idea behind this book really started while I was working as a green coffee buyer. While I was on the phone with an importer, getting more information about a coffee in which our company was interested, the sales representative told me a story about the producer of the coffee: the farmer was an 80-something-year-old widow who was continuing her late husband's legacy as a coffee farmer and was thriving in her work. Her son would drive her around the lots to check on the plants, and he would run the day-to-day operations. They would pay top wages to the workers they hired, so high that the workers chose to stay in the area year round instead of search for work in neighboring countries throughout the season. If a worker was injured while on the job and couldn't work as a result, instead of letting his family go without money, the son would pay out something similar to a life insurance policy to make sure that the bills would be paid, medical expenses would be covered, and life could continue on as normal. Hearing that about someone halfway across the world ignited within me a passion to teach others about what goes on behind the scenes of the coffee industry that may not be evident to the consumer. It's kept me going through the tough interactions with difficult customers, and has provided me with fuel to keep telling this farmer's story to every coffee curious person I meet.

As a result of this, what you'll find in this volume is a compilation of acquired insights, concepts, and tricks that make coffee and the expansive backstory it has more palatable (no pun intended). You will find answers to questions like, "What really is coffee, and where does it come from?" You will have some ammunition in your pocket that you can use next time you are in line at both your local coffee shop and the large corporate chain stores that can be found on almost every corner. You will (hopefully) be able to make informed decisions when it comes to buying your next bag of beans. And, what I hope to be most helpful about this book, you will have the tools to make a better cup of coffee when you finish the last page.

When you begin to apply what you have read here, please do not get discouraged if you make mistakes in the brewing (or purchasing) process. The best way to learn better about what you are attempting is to have failures along the way. I have spent many mornings scratching my head and asking myself why the cup of coffee I just made, using all the recipes and tips that I know, tastes less than delicious. It's all one big journey: the farther along you find yourself on the journey, the more you realize that you still have so much to learn. That is completely okay. Proceed down the caffeinated path with the understanding that you will grow and improve each time you touch coffee.

With that, I wish you happy brewing, happy learning, and happy growing.

How To Use This Book

This book is divided into three sections: Before You Drink, How To Drink Now, and How To Drink Later. You'll be equipped with both theoretical and practical information both for understanding concepts you may hear once or twice and for applying your new-found knowledge in your everyday life. The most optimal (and intended) use is to trace the journey from start to finish: how coffee gets from the farm to your countertop, whether in whole bean or drink form.

The first section, Before You Drink, is great for doubling down on your coffee education. Use the footnotes to do more research in the cited sources, and keep studying.

The second section, How To Drink Now, is what you can take with you into your normal coffee stop tomorrow morning. Observe the differences wherever you go, and try your hand at making your own coffee with a new bag of beans.

The third section, How To Drink Later, is best practice for how to keep your coffee fresher longer. Your coffee will change over time, but you can take steps to prevent premature aging.

Part One: Before You Drink

What Exactly Is Coffee?

My personal belief/way of operation, especially when it comes to things that interest me, is to dig into the origins, myths, and details behind different topics. When I first started out in the coffee industry, I knew little to nothing about coffee; all it was to me was a hot (or sometimes cold) liquid that kept me somewhere between staying awake and feeling jittery. But, when I dug further into what coffee really is, where it comes from, and what it means to the world around me, it really struck a chord in me. Contrary to popular belief, coffee doesn't start out as a brown bean. It doesn't even start out as just a bean. What coffee really is is a seed, more like a pit, found in the middle of a coffee fruit; the fruit resembles a cherry tomato, and is often referred to as a cherry within the coffee world.

Another interesting fact to note: coffee isn't native to the USA[1]. Coffee trees are generally grown in tropical regions, quite literally between the Tropic Of Cancer and Tropic Of Capricorn (between 25° N and 30° S, for all you geography nerds out there like myself). Whether it be from South/Central America, Africa, or Asia, coffee trees require a specific climate in which to grow, mature, and produce properly formed fruit.

Thing Of Legend

Coffee isn't a 20th century discovery, or even a considerably modern find. Coffee consumption in some form dates back to possibly the 9th century, beginning with the legend of Kaldi and his dancing goats[2]. The myth states that Kaldi, an Ethiopian goatherder, noticed his goats snacking on a fruit tree that kept them full of energy. So, in order to see what the fuss was, and what kept them going back to the tree time and time again, he decided to try the fruit for himself.

---

[1] Within the past 3 years, farmers like Jay Ruskey in Goleta, California, have begun attempting to grow coffee trees and have found success. This is the exception to the rule. I tried my hand at growing a coffee tree in Middle Tennessee while I was writing this guide. Long story short, it failed, both because of the climate and because I do not possess a green thumb.

[2] Bennett Alan Weinberg, PH.D., and Bonnie K. Bealer. *The World of Caffeine: The Science and Culture of the World's Most Popular Drug* (New York: Routledge, 2002), 3-4.

He felt more energized than he had after eating other fruits, so he brought some to an Islamic holy man. The holy man was no fan of these fruits, and in disgust threw them in the fire. Lo and behold, the fruit began to give off a pleasing aroma, so the pair gathered them from the embers, ground them up, and let them dissolve in hot water.

This myth has caused a wave of excitement within the coffee community, and rightfully so; it's a fun little tale for baristas to tell curious customers who are interested in learning a little more about the coffee they're drinking. It engages and evokes a wonder about a product to which most consumers have paid such little attention. In the grand scheme of things, there is no concrete historical evidence that this story has any factual backing. The story itself didn't appear until roughly 1671, when Antoine Faustus Nairon published one of the earliest writings about coffee[3]. The biggest takeaway concerning the stories behind coffee and its origin is that it goes beyond our Americanized and commoditized view of the beverage that has become a cultural phenomenon. It dates back to a time before the modern era, and has made generations of people both gaze in awe and shake their fists in frustration at all facets of the coffee making process.

---

[3] *Ibid.*, 3-4.

In Its Element

So, now that we've established from where coffee originated in history, we can move to the next phase of what exactly coffee is, and how it gets from where it is to our local coffee shop. As previously stated, coffee grows on trees and looks something like a cherry tomato. It grows best at high altitudes in regions with tropical climates: temperatures that average above 65° F with considerable rainfall year round. Therefore, we can assume that coffee is not a native plant to the USA, which is why roasters must import their coffee in order to serve it in cafés and shops across the country.

Coffee also has different plant species within the larger umbrella of its taxonomy. Just as apples come in different varieties, such as Granny Smith, Gala, Golden Delicious, etc., so do coffee plants. Coffee varieties determine different factors in the growing process, such as plant height, survivability in the wild, difficulty of cultivation, and frequency of fruit production. The different varieties also garner a variety of pricing standards in the market, based on the supply and demand across the world.

There have been many wiser men and women who have undertaken the task of writing at length about the coffee plant, best practice for growing coffee, and the germination, maturation, and flowering of the crop. These individuals are infinitely smarter than I am, and I would be unwise to steal away any bravado from their published works. This guide, however, is not a comprehensive botany and agricultural work, so in an effort not to bore you, I won't write much further about the minute details surrounding the coffee plant itself.

But, it is important to note that coffee farming is nothing short of a lesson in patience, observation, and trust; most coffee plants take between 3 to 4 years to reach the point where they are producing usable fruit. This also means that coffee farmers may not see the return on their investment for years. Before workers can pick ripe fruit from the plants, the farmers carefully monitor the progress of the trees, ensuring that pests, forces of nature, and soil content do not prevent the tree from performing its best.

But, once the harvest season begins and the farmers see usable crop, the picking commences. Whether picked mechanically or by hand (both have their benefits), ripe coffee cherries begin the journey to their final destination as they leave the tree and enter into the processing phase.

Trust The Process(ing)

Picked cherries have multiple layers that make up the fruit. Just like an avocado has the skin, the pit, and the main reason for buying an avocado (something I'll refer to as the pulp of the fruit throughout this section, mainly in reference to coffee), so coffee cherries have skin, pulp, seeds, and more that compose the make up of this fascinating little fruit. However, unlike an avocado where the pulp is most desirable, the most desirable part of the coffee cherry is, in fact, the seed.

These cherries must go through a series of steps in order to get down to just the seed of the fruit, which is most commonly known as the bean. But, there are a few different methods by which cherries can be processed; the three main methods that deal with how farmers strip away the outer layers of the fruit are *washed*, *natural*, and *honey*. All have their advantages on both sides of the supply chain, and all have different contributions to the final taste of the bean once it goes through roasting.

In as concise a way as possible, let's look at what happens in each method[4]:

Washed Process

This is the most intensive of the processes, yet also the process that yields the most consistent final product. Picked cherries go into floatation tanks, allowing ripe and unripe cherries to separate from one another. Ripe cherries float, while unripe sink to the bottom. Depulpers remove the skin and pulp mechanically in order to expose the seed. The seeds then go into fermentation tanks to remove any excess pulp. From the fermentation tanks, seeds go into another washing tank as a final precaution to remove any leftover residue. The process concludes with the seeds being laid out to dry either on raised beds to increase air exposure or on patios, being regularly turned to promote even drying across the selection of beans. As a result of the multiple steps in the process, washed coffees typically have cleaner tasting notes and uniformity across the beans from the lot.

---

[4] Most of my knowledge concerning processing comes from James Hoffman's *The World Atlas Of Coffee*. The proceeding descriptions are summaries from his section on processing (pp.31-37).

Natural Process

This is the simplest of the processes, containing the fewest steps in among the major processing methods. Workers hand sort picked cherries after harvest, and immediately lay them out in the sun either on patios or raised beds. Workers rake cherries in order to ensure even air and sun exposure. This process is most popular in areas where water is not readily accessible, such as Ethiopia and Brazil. Natural processed coffees typically have fruitier flavor profiles, regardless of the surrounding plant life, soil content, and variety.

Honey Process

This is, in my opinion, the more unique processing method, since it blends steps from the previous two processes to create a sweeter final product. Depending on the location, the honey process has different names: pulped natural, *miel*, and semi-washed or wet-hulled. Each specific method under the honey processing umbrella exists for different reasons, whether as a conservation effort or an experiment to hybridize the two most common methods. The picked cherries go into flotation tanks to separate ripe from unripe cherries, like in the washed process. The ripe cherries then go through the depulper to remove the skin and most of the flesh. Then, instead of going into fermentation tanks, the depulped cherries go straight to the patio or drying bed. Without the thicker layer of pulp around the seed, drying times for the cherries increases, which also increase perceived sweetness and cup body.

An Import(ant) Step

While there are a few more steps in the processing phase, they all amount to what comes next: shipping, and ultimately importing into the destination country. Once processing is completed, the beans, also known as green coffee, go into a resting period, which sets up the product for optimal aging and a longer window of freshness once packaged, and usually takes between one and two months. After the beans have rested, they go through mechanical hulling, which removes the remaining parchment-like layer surrounding the green coffee. Once hulled, the beans are evaluated and graded[5] in order to communicate quality to potential buyers before the beans leave the farm.

---

[5] SCA (Specialty Coffee Association) defines grade as, "Quality designation for coffee beans. Criteria for determining grade include size, density, altitude, and number of defects (such as twigs, stones, bugs, under- or overripe beans) per pound. Generally the best beans are graded A, AA, AAA, or grade one. Next is A grade, AB grade, X grade and Y grade."

Typically, shipping coffee takes a substantial amount of time from country of origin to the destination country. Producers ship coffee in large containers via container ships (since air freight still remains a more expensive method of transport), which sometimes takes weeks to get from point A to point B. Factor in that most exporting countries hold up coffee shipments due to bureaucratic, paperwork-laden processes, and the timeline expands even further.

From entering into the destination country, at least in America, coffee either goes to an importer's warehouse, a shared warehouse, or directly into the roaster's possession. Some importers, like Cafe Imports and Anthem Imports, have their own space to house green coffee and distribute it as needed. Either way, proper storage is key for keeping green coffee fresh, so the right mix of temperature, humidity, light exposure, and monitoring makes for the most optimal location for keeping green coffee ready to roast.

From growing to importing, coffee takes a massive journey before it ever reaches our hands. It's something that we take for granted and don't consider when we look at bags on the shelves, cups of piping hot coffee, and baristas working hard to make drinks for customers. When we take into account how far beyond ourselves coffee really is, we recognize the beauty and wonder that amounts to one of the most popular drinks in the world. But, the journey that coffee takes doesn't end here; this is purely in reference to un-roasted coffee. When coffee is roasted, a whole new segment of the journey begins.

What Happens In Roasting?

Green coffee cannot be consumed in its raw form, at least not enjoyably. The beans have a straw-like, rubbery taste that isn't pleasant to sip on for an extended period of time. So, green coffee must be processed in order to be happily and readily consumable. As we learned within the legend of Kaldi and his dancing goats, a more desirable way to use the beans is through baking, also known as roasting, and dissolving the crushed roasted beans in hot water. One of the ways that the modern coffee movement has brought out the intricacies found in the processing phase is through carefully roasting these beans and monitoring the process through data collection and research.

Roasting coffee is one of the lesser understood components in the coffee industry; too few people want to dedicate the time and energy to learning this trade. And, in all reality, training to roast coffee is an expensive process. But, when grasped, the concepts within the craft are invaluable and beautiful to see come together as the roast progresses, especially once you taste the final product.

Truth be told: roasting and all its philosophies can be downright boring. While I may nerd out about a smooth roasting curve, it very well might be putting dozens of people to sleep as I bring it up in casual conversation. But, in some degree, I believe it's important to have a basic understanding of what really goes into a given roast so that you can at least carry on a decent conversation at your local café. You may never stand behind a roaster in your life, but having a working knowledge of what happens in each portion of the roast paints a better picture as to why you might be tasting certain flavors in your coffee.

I don't expect you to become an expert on roasting theory or the chemistry involved in the process just by reading this chapter. There's always more that you can learn, and there's always more to unlock within the roasting process. What follows is an abbreviated set of descriptions of the different major benchmarks within a given roast.

The Phases Of Roasting

There are three main phases that happen while coffee is in the roaster: drying, Maillard, and development. And each portion is marked off by key events such as turning point, color change, first crack, and (if roasted long enough) second crack. Each phase plays a crucial role in bringing out perceived body, clarity, acidity, sweetness, and brightness once someone brews a cup of coffee. The most trained palate may be able to notice in one sip that the beans spent too much time within Maillard, didn't have enough time to develop, or dried out too fast before hitting color change.

Drying

Bringing a virtually non-consumable bean to the point where flavors are popping left and right takes quite a bit of work. Green coffee is roughly 10%-15% moisture content, depending on who you ask, and that moisture content must be removed from the mix in order to bring about the chemical reactions that make coffee what it is. The phase name gives away exactly what's going on: the coffee beans, once dropped into the roaster, begin a process of drying in order to prepare for further development within the structure of the coffee. This phase sets up your roast for success. If you dry a batch of coffee too fast due to too much heat energy being created, you may have to spend more time than desired slowing down the momentum and could end up with what's called a runaway roast: the temperature rises too high, too fast. If you dry a batch of coffee too slow due to not enough heat energy being created, you may end up playing catch up later on in the roast, leaving you to introduce too much heat too late.

Once drying phase finishes, roasters mark the end of the phase by designating *color change*. The color of the beans quite literally changes from a dull green to a pale yellow, which can be observed through the roaster's glass port. As color change occurs, the next phase of the roast begins.

Maillard Phase

After color change, the beans are primed and ready to go through the main portion of transformation, where the majority of the flavor profile of the coffee develops and shines. The phase is named after Louis-Camille Maillard, a French chemist who first recognized the chemical reactions between amino acids and sugars while attempting to reproduce biological protein synthesis. Scott Rao, author of *The Coffee Roaster's Companion*, defines what happens in Maillard as, "[N]onenzymatic browning reactions between free amino acids and reducing sugars, and they contribute to coffee's brown color, bittersweet flavor, and various aromas"[1]. In simplified terms, everything that we've come to know and love about coffee really does

---

[1] Scott Rao. *The Coffee Roaster's Companion* (Scott Rao, 2014), 17.

happen in the Maillard phase. Now, there are hundreds of chemical reactions happening within the beans, since the temperature within the roaster is continually rising and different reactions happen at different temperatures. But, this phase really boils down to creating the foundational changes that set the stage for the coffee to shine.

Once Maillard finishes, roasters mark the end of the phase with what's called *first crack*; there is an audible series of pops that occur within the roaster. First crack happens as the beans release any leftover moisture content, now present as water vapor, and carbon dioxide that's been produced throughout the roast. This marker usually occurs about 75% of the way through the roast, transitioning the beans into the next phase.

Development Phase

After first crack occurs, the final phase of roasting begins. While all along the roast the beans have been going through development, this phase really marks the polishing and finalization of internal bean development. Most roasters manipulate these factors based on desired roast level. The longer you keep beans in development phase, the more baked or "roasty" the coffee will taste. Roasters will usually mark progress and quality of the roast by the percentage of time spent in development, sometimes even priding themselves on the consistency and brevity of their development phases if they're roasting coffee to a lighter profile.

There are two next steps that can occur while in development: you can either finish the roast and keep the coffee profile at a medium roast, or continue to *second crack*[2]. Pressure starts to build again within the bean core, and oils that were trapped in the bean structure are able to release to the exterior. Roasters should be careful to monitor bean progress post-second crack, since going too far past this marker may result in carbon-like notes in the cup, as well as unpleasant body when drinking the product.

There Are Levels To This Stuff

Now that we have a basic understanding of the different benchmarks, it's important to describe what each roast level brings along with it as it pertains to taste notes, perceived body, acidity, and sweetness. When discussing the flavor profile of coffee, you can get any level of strength out of any kind of roast; we'll cover that a little

---

[2] To my knowledge, most specialty coffee roasters won't go to second crack. Second crack is usually an indicator of a dark roasted coffee, and as of late, very few people within the specialty coffee community really enjoy coffee with the flavor implications that the profile has.

later in the book, but it's important to note that as we discuss roast levels since many people associated how light or dark a roast is with how weak or strong a coffee is.

Different roasters have different definitions of roast levels. It's confusing, and makes everyone's job harder when describing coffees to customers who may be used to another local roaster's products, or even a larger corporation's coffees (which honestly all taste the same, in my opinion). The light-medium roast I produce day in and day out might be a very light roast to you, or the medium roast you brew daily might be a dark roast to me. The language within the coffee industry is currently unequal, but we'll look at the roast levels with a general description that applies to local specialty coffee roasteries.

Light Roast

This level of roast is marked by its higher yet pleasant acidity, clear yet distinguishable taste notes, medium body, and sweetness as the coffee cools. When observing the beans, they resemble the coloration of a milk chocolate bar and have what look like wrinkles on the back. As you grind the beans, the fragrance is pronounced and has a generally sweet smell.

Medium Roast

This level of roast is marked by its smooth and less prevalent acidity, balanced flavor profile, sometimes heavier body that isn't unpleasant, and often robust aroma. When observing the beans, they take on a lower percentage dark chocolate bar coloration and slight wrinkled texture. As you grind the beans, the fragrance is slightly muted yet has cocoa-like notes.

Dark Roast

This level of roast is marked by its bittersweet notes, syrupy mouthfeel, carbon-like aromas, and minute acidity. With such extended times spent in development, most flavors that might be present in lighter roasts are cooked out and replaced by often burnt and smoky flavors. When observing the beans, the exterior may have a shiny, glossy finish due to oils and resemble a higher percentage, almost completely dark dark chocolate bar. As you grind the beans, the fragrance is dominated by smoky tobacco-like notes.

Without going through the roasting process, the raw coffee product we bring into the shop wouldn't be deemed as consumable. However intricate, and altogether confusing, roasting may be, this is a place where art and science collide to create something that can make the work of a farmer shine bright. No matter how light or dark you prefer your coffee, there's a reason why your coffee is the way it is, and for that reason alone it makes the art of roasting coffee beautiful.

Part Two: How To Drink Now

How Do I Order At A Coffee Shop?

If you've made it this far in the book, congratulations. The hard, dense, and relatively academic subject matter is over and done with. The theory chapter is closed, and you can breathe a sigh of relief. Now, we get to have fun with what we just discussed and can actually apply those concepts in our everyday lives. Not every coffee shop you walk into will share information about their roasting; the producers who supplied their beans, whether by direct trade relationships or through importers; or even best practices with how to order what you want at the register. That's really annoying to me, and at some places, it keeps me from wanting to visit again.

Just like I mentioned with different shops having different meanings and understandings for how light or dark a roast is, there currently is no common language within the coffee industry as to what defines drink size, drink type, or syrup level additions. Now, this is one thing about which many people agree has a common root source, and that's the introduction of corporate-run coffee chains. No I will not use names, or speak down about these large scale operations. Whether we want to admit it or not, these chains created a gateway to and curiosity concerning deeper coffee concepts with the plethora of menu items they offer.

However, these menu items are not synonymous across the larger coffee industry spectrum. Specialty coffee shops use different verbiage to describe their drinks than the larger corporations. You can't expect to get the same thing you order from a green apron-wearing barista when you're in a locally-owned upscale café, and vice versa. It's created enough confusion for baristas who may have left the chains to find other coffee education avenues, and it's something we need to address before moving forward with best practices of how to order at the coffee shops you plan on visiting. The traditional definitions and understandings of drinks are most widely used at local coffee shops, but may carry different meanings elsewhere.

Macchiato

Why not start things off with a bang, right? This is by far one of the most confusing offerings in a coffee shop. One place defines it as an upside down latte that comes in varying sizes; another defines it as a double shot of espresso with foam on top. Within the specialty coffee realm, if you order a macchiato in a local shop, you're most likely going to receive a very small cup (or a mostly empty cup if you're taking it to go). A good, hospitable barista should ask if you're looking for a traditional or "modern," otherwise known as chain, selection, but unfortunately not everyone is trained to dig deeper. Traditional macchiatos do only come in one size, so be aware of that as you order them. The word *macchiato* in Italian means, "Marked," so a traditional macchiato is espresso marked with semi-dry foam.

Cappuccino

While not as confusing as a macchiato, cappuccinos have a reputation of being finicky to order, coming with all sorts of modifications: extra dry, light foam, with or without syrups, etc. The chains have multiple sizes, but local shops usually offer them in a specific, smaller size. With all of this difference, what really is a cappuccino?

Traditionally, cappuccinos are made up of three equally separated components: one part espresso, one part steamed milk, one part foam. They're usually served in a six ounce cup, where the foam is scooped out on top of the drink instead of incorporated with the steamed milk. Most specialty coffee shops will serve cappuccinos more like an Australian *flat white* (which is essentially a short latte) and will incorporate the foam in order to pour art onto the surface. Chains, however, will serve cappuccino-style lattes in their main size offerings, making the drink extra dry and scooping the foam on top of the milk. Traditional cappuccinos are also steamed to a lower temperature than lattes, bringing out the natural sweetness of the milk. It's a great drink for the coffee lover who enjoys milk-based drinks, but only wants a little milk with their espresso.

Latte

Now, this is one of the most universal offerings across the coffee spectrum: espresso with steamed milk, with a light layer of foam. You can request no foam, extra foam, extra hot, etc., and it's easily understood how to fulfill your wishes. It generally transcends sizes, which makes it so easy to get the same thing time and time again. But, where the differentiation between chain and local shops occurs is the exact ratio of espresso to milk: some serve it with a double shot no matter what size, and some add additional shots the larger you go. Either way, it's imperative that your barista offer an explanation if the ratio changes at a given point on the latte menu.

If you order a latte at a local shop, you're more than likely going to receive a nice little white heart, leaf, or flower on the top of your drink.

This is a nice little touch that I personally enjoy adding, but the way the drink is structured as a result is important to note. The steamed milk, containing enough foam to create a base, dilutes the espresso so that the concentrated shot expands across the milk, providing the right structure to support the latte art to be poured. The milk helps tame the strong "coffee" taste of the espresso while also allowing the tasting notes to shine forth against the background of the milk.

Mocha

While a mocha is technically a latte with some form of chocolate syrup, it can get a little tricky knowing what you're getting yourself into depending on the shop from which you're ordering one. Even in the local shop realm, there's a distinct possibility that a mocha from one could be different from another. You might take a sip from the shop on the east side of town and get a rich, dark chocolate ganache mixed into your latte. You might get a milkier chocolate sauce mixed into your drink from the one downtown. Or, the chain down the street from your house might serve it to you with a mountain of whipped cream.

As you consider ordering a mocha, make sure to ask the right questions, the ones that matter to you: what kind of chocolate is in the mocha? Does it normally come with or without whip? How much syrup is being mixed into the drink? Is it mixed into the espresso, or into the milk? Either way, it's important that you know what chocolatey treat you're about to order.

Blended Drinks

So, this is one of those items that differentiates a specialty coffee shop from a corporate chain: can you order a frozen drink that comes from a blender? In my experience, you'll rarely find a local specialty shop that blends drinks as a frozen option. It could be for many reasons as to why these shops choose not to have blended drinks as a part of the menu, but one thing remains constant: these drinks are not fun to make. It interrupts the barista bar flow, it's loud, it takes away from the flavors of the coffee, and it takes forever to clean, among other complaints.

One thing to be careful about when ordering a blended drink at a corporate chain location: these drinks may contain more sugar than coffee. While the standard customer who regularly orders these drinks may not be the most coffee savvy guest, and may prefer the sugar high that mimics the effects of caffeine, these options are more like an after-dinner dessert instead of first cup of the morning.

Ordering With Purpose

As you're standing in front of the register, you're faced with so many options. Do you want a lot of milk? Do you want something with espresso? Or just black coffee? Do you want it hot or iced? How much do you want to drink? Or do you just ask the barista what he or she really likes? The list of questions you have to answer goes on and on and on, seemingly without end. It feels like you're in a real life choose-your-own-adventure book. Frankly, you really are; ordering coffee *is* an exciting adventure that can be enjoyable if you order with purpose. There are some basic questions you need to ask yourself each time that you want to order a drink. No matter from where you choose to purchase coffee, I guarantee you'll find the drink for you after you answer these inquiries.

Drink Temperature

Most shops offer both hot and iced options for the majority of the menu. Your first decision needs to be if you're interested in something that's cold or something that's hot. This first question helps you proceed toward the next step with confidence.

Espresso Vs. Filter Coffee

Now that you've figured out if you want hot or iced, now you get to figure out the kind of coffee you'll be drinking. The two main types of coffee options are espresso and filter coffee, otherwise known as brewed coffee. With espresso options, there are further levels of consideration that we'll cover next. But, with filter coffee, you end up having two main options: drip or iced/cold brew.

Drink Size

Typically, in espresso based options, drink sizes come with their own names. Cortados (one part espresso, one part steamed milk) are four ounces, cappuccinos (one part espresso, one part steamed milk, one part foam) are six ounces, and lattes (two ounces of espresso plus remaining contents filled with steamed milk) are eight and 12 ounces (or even 16 and above, especially in iced sizes). In filter coffee options, drip coffee comes in two main sizes (8/12 ounces) and iced coffee/cold brew in one main size (16 ounces).

Milk Content

When it comes to espresso, you do have an important decision to make concerning how much milk you want, and even what kind of milk. The size of your espresso-based drink determines the milk content; if you want a little bit of milk in your hot drink, go with a cortado, which is equal parts steamed milk and espresso. If you want a lot of milk, then whether you're drinking it hot or iced, go with a large latte.

Concerning filter based drinks, a little bit of milk goes a long way. Whether you add half and half, whole milk, or almond/oat milk, the coloration of the filter coffee changes readily with the slightest amount of addition. Make sure you're monitoring the taste as you add milk or creamer so that you aren't over-diluting your drink!

Sweetness/Syrup Level

While I'm a purist concerning syrups and sweeteners, I can appreciate a little extra flavoring every now and then. It can mask certain unappealing flavors in drinks, as well as enhance pleasant flavors. But, there's a fine line between just enough and too much in the syrup realm. When it comes to espresso based drinks that have flavors in them, ask your barista what unit of measure they're using when preparing the drink. Many shops will use ounces or grams to be as precise as possible, but there are still a group that will use either tablespoon scoops or large chain-style pumps. Understanding the measurements at play will help you decide whether or not you need less (or more) syrup than what comes standard. You can't always taste the sweetness level considered standard before ordering to determine how sweet the drink will be, so proceed with caution.

When it comes to filter based drinks, it's easier to determine your desired sweetness level in increments and taste it along the way. No matter where you are, give your drink a chance before you add anything to it. It sounds risky, but you may find out you love black coffee just like I do.

If you find yourself not sure what to order at your local coffee shop, ask the barista what their favorite drink is (and ask them what's in it, just to be safe). Treat them like experts, since they're the ones making drinks day in and day out for other customers. But, knowing how different places go about making drinks that other places might make differently is half the battle when ordering your coffee. The power of your daily pick-me-up is ultimately in your hands, after all.

How Do I Pick Beans To Bring Home With Me?

One of the more exciting parts of a coffee shop experience comes when you get to the retail shelves. I enjoy looking at the options these places have for bringing coffee home with me to recreate the delicious cup of coffee I just finished drinking (or sometimes, to try and make it better myself). Most shops offer multiple options for whole bean coffee, hailing from different regions with a variety of processing methods and more confusing information that doesn't always make sense. Why do these roasters put so many words and numbers on these labels when all I want to do is drink coffee at home? The reality is that what you're reading on the bag is actually pretty simple to understand. Just like with any coffee idea, you can go as deep into your research as you want and find out what certain pieces of information means for the chemistry, taste, and the producers, but making informed decisions on your purchase based on what you're seeing on the label is easy.

Appropriately Labeled

As I continue to look through other roasters' selections and see what they're sharing concerning coffees, everyone wants to display transparency and integrity with the products they're selling. And I love it. But, not everyone understands what's so important about listing MASL (meters above sea level) when it comes to coffee development, or what a roast date means for coffee freshness. While this data is listed to help consumers continue their coffee journey, it isn't always possible when the necessary tools aren't available from the roaster themselves.

Typically, when you look on the label, you'll find this information: country, region, farm/producer, varietal(s), process, elevation, and taste notes. Roasters use these descriptions to give you a preview of what you're about to drink. Different countries and regions produce different flavor profiles for coffee, just as wine tastes differently from region to region. Different elevations allow the coffee plants to grow in different ways. And, just as we discussed earlier, different processes produce different kinds of notes. All in all, the information you see listed gives you a window into what makes the beans unique.

Country/Region

The biggest deciding factor (outside the listed taste notes) when choosing coffee usually is the country or region from where it originated. Seeing if a coffee is a Yirgacheffe from Ethiopia, or a Nariño from Colombia, will draw in even the least informed customer while looking over the coffee selection. And it makes sense; each country typically has an overarching flavor profile. Central American coffees are chocolatey and nutty, even citrusy, and Eastern African coffees are fruity and sweet. Depending on the regions within the countries, different types of fruit or chocolate might be more prevalent too. So, as you read the labels and see different regions, you'll be able to figure out what kind of tastes you'll find starting with the country of origin.

Farm/Producer

If the roaster cares about traceability and transparency, the next piece of information you'll find is the name of the farm and/or the name of producer, sometimes even the washing or processing station, from where the coffee was grown and prepared for export. While this information is arguably extraneous and may not mean much, it does help communicate that coffee goes much further than roasters and cafés. There's always a story attached to a farmer, which I believe is important to consider when we as coffee professionals import coffees and describe them to consumers. When you compare different roasters' options and see the same farm and producer information listed as offerings at two or more shops, you can have some fun evaluating which roaster's handling of the bean you prefer.

Varietal(s)

Just as I mentioned in the first chapter, coffee comes in different varieties, just like apples. Each varietal has a different genetic make up, which ultimately determines how the plants themselves will grow. Different plant characteristics, like plant height, distance between leaves, and distance between fruit on the plant, will ultimately affect the way the beans taste when roasted. You may have seen somewhere on a coffee bag something like *Typica*, *Castillo*, *Pacamara*, *Maraogype*, *Bourbon*, or even *Gesha/Geisha*. All of those are technically species of coffee plants. These varietals often come with price differentials, since they vary in plant cost, cost of upkeep & cultivation, and cost of production, as well as where these species are grown. Certain varietals, like *Castillo* and *Colombia*, are natives to

Central/South America, while varietals like *Typica* can grow almost anywhere.

Since the early 2000's, one varietal in particular has gained quite a momentum within the coffee industry. The *Gesha/Geisha* species of coffee is highly sought after by roasters, since the varietal is rare and often expensive. Yielding high citrus acidity, unique fruit notes, and an often tea-like body, there is nothing quite like a *Gesha*. Originating in Ethiopia, the species has been propagated and cultivated across the world, yielding top dollar for each crop on the market. The most well-known Gesha producer is Hacienda La Esmerelda in Panama, which started the craze over the species in 2004; the coffee auctioned at the time for $21/pound, which was unheard of in the coffee buying world. Over the years, the prices of their harvest went up, hovering at around $50/pound. In 2017, Hacienda La Esmerelda auctioned a coffee for $601/pound, and a neighboring *Gesha* farm, Lamastus Family Estates, auctioned a coffee for $803/pound the following year.

All that to say, varietals are an important part of the decision making process when choosing a coffee to buy. Understanding and identifying the varietals on the coffees you've liked in the past will help you to narrow your search results, and give you a frame of reference when you see a catalog of offerings that have these species listed.

Process

In addition to the varietals/species of the coffee used to roast up a batch, processing notes play a major part in how a coffee tastes as well. Earlier, we looked briefly at the three main processes used in coffee production, and this is where that information comes into practical use. Most roasters will pride themselves on their offerings being a certain process, especially when it comes to a really good natural or a specially chosen washed. While natural coffees will ultimately have heavy berry-focused notes, washed coffees take a little extra care and finesse to hone in on the flavors. Not every washed coffee will display traditional chocolate or cherry notes, and working with the processes used to prepare coffee for consumption is how roasters can imprint their own signature onto the product.

Natural processed coffees, while still being fruity and sweet, will also differ in taste focuses from country to country. A natural Guatemalan (which, in my opinion, is a work of art) will ultimately display a different set of fruit flavors than a natural Ethiopian. While natural coffees have a bad reputation in certain coffee circles, if you tend to like more unique flavors in your coffee, you can easily find what you're looking for in a natural offering.

Within the honey processing realm, you might get the chance to see roasters list a color level with the offering; the main color distinctions of honey processes are white, yellow, red, and black honey. As you see these on bags, the color level correlates to how much of the pulp was left on the seed while it was drying. White is the least amount of pulp, while black is the most amount of pulp without being a full natural. Below is a diagram with approximations of pulp level, including washed and natural processed coffee levels for reference.

PROCESSING METHOD	PULP PRESENT WHEN DRYING (%)
Washed	0%
White Honey	1-25%
Yellow Honey	26-50%
Red Honey	51-75%
Black Honey	76-99%
Natural	100%

Also, if you're having a hard time deciding between processes, it never hurts to ask a barista for recommendations. They get to work with the coffees day in and day out, and they know what's tasting great, and what needs a little more time to develop and grow within the roasting realm.

Elevation

Listing elevation may seem irrelevant to your coffee drinking experience, but there's validity to displaying the information. The elevation on the bag describes how high or low the coffee was grown, and this has some interesting implications on the taste, genetics, and structure of the beans. Ultimately, within the industry, there is an understanding that higher elevations produce higher quality coffees. If you compare the notes between a coffee grown above 1200 meters (4000ft) with one grown at 750 meters (~2400ft), you'll notice that the higher altitude coffees have fruitier, sweeter notes, which is generally more desirable than earthier, grassy notes from lower altitude coffees. Roasters who list this altitude information will usually have a list of offerings that stay within a 1200m-2100m range, which produces flavors like chocolate, cherry, berry, and assorted fruits.

Elevation also influences how coffee on the tree matures and grows. At lower elevations, oxygen is more prevalent, which means the plants can go through aerobic respiration using the air around them for energy and produce fruit more frequently. However, at higher elevations, oxygen is more scarce, which forces the plants to go through anaerobic respiration and use other means of energy production; typically, lactic acid is broken down in order to create the energy needed to produce fruit. The process is slower, but, with more time to develop the characteristics and profile associated with the higher elevations, the payoff ends up being higher for the producer and roaster.

Taste Notes

All of the information listed on the bag comes to a culmination in one final listing: taste notes. The taste notes end up being the final say in whether someone buys a coffee or not. Think of the tasting notes as a dependent variable in the coffee equation, essentially. And with taste being so subjective and personal, there truly is a coffee out there for everyone. Tasting notes can vary between *traditional*, which includes chocolate, cocoa/cacao, and burnt sugar, and *modern*, which includes berry, sweet fruit, and syrups like molasses and maple.

Taste notes are meant to be more of a guide and target than a hard and fast rule; what tastes like blueberry to one person might taste like chocolate to another person, and that could just be on the third day off-roast. As coffee ages, the taste could alter in both good and bad ways. Brewing variables, such as water temperature, grind size, water chemistry, and agitation, will ultimately affect how coffee tastes, and could end up making or breaking your cup of joe. So, be mindful of how your coffee is tasting as you brew through the bag. You have the power in your hands to make your coffee taste either good or bad.

Taking your favorite coffee shop home with you in the form of a bag of beans can help to continue the great experience you had day in and day out. Roasters try their hardest to give you a product that will brighten your day, give you a pep in your step, and give you reason to come back once the bag is done. Using the listed information on the labels, you can carefully take your daily routine from average to extraordinary. You can either stick within your comfort zone of flavors that you know you like, or you can experiment with unique taste notes that you would never expect.

How Should I Brew This Coffee?

We've touched on so much of the coffee journey thus far. Most of it has been theoretical, at least in the vein of taking the information in before applying it. But, now that you've brought home beans with you, what do you do with them? How do you recreate that great cup of coffee that inspired you to purchase the bag in the first place? What we'll be focusing on in this chapter is making the best cup of coffee you can while at home, and finding the tools you need to help you in the process. Brewing coffee at home can be just as much a therapeutic act as it is a kickstart to your day. In my experience, while I've been preparing my first cup of the day, it seems like everything around me pauses while I focus on what I'm doing in the brewing process. It helps me recenter my mind before the busyness of the day begins, and allows me to step into that day's task list calmly and intentionally, as well as properly caffeinated and fueled.

Tools For The Work

If you sit around a coffee shop long enough, you know that even professionals can't make cups of coffee appear out of thin air (even though it seems like sometimes with how fast they're moving). And the same goes for the home barista as well. It sounds like a given, but in order to brew coffee at home, there are a few key pieces of equipment that you need. Even the least expensive Mr. Coffee grinder and coffee maker go a long way for preparing coffee fresh. You don't have to break the bank on equipment either; while the pricier options like Baratza might produce a more precise grind or have a more intricate process, brands like Capresso and Bodum have reasonably priced options that will give you exactly what you're looking for in a day-in-day-out product that you can purchase at Target or Bed, Bath, & Beyond.

Regardless of the price point, I believe there are a few pieces of equipment that you need to ensure you're getting the best cup of coffee: a brewer with a decanter/pot, a grinder, a scale, a timer, and/or a gooseneck kettle (depending on if you choose to get an automatic brewer). Obviously, having a brewing device, like a basic coffee maker or pour over set up, is a must in brewing coffee, unless you go the route of cowboy coffee and want to boil very coarsely ground beans on the stovetop. The brewer serves as the backbone and starting point of any coffee making venture.

What's equally as important is a grinder at home. I highly recommend grinding your coffee on-demand instead of having your local coffee shop grind it for you[1]. There are two main types of grinders: blade and burr. Blade grinders work similarly to blenders; there's a single spinning blade that grinds the beans for as long as you hold down the "on" button. While their price point is significantly lower than burr grinders, blade grinders typically produce a non-uniform grind that can greatly affect coffee brewing. These are best used when implementing immersion-based brew methods, like a french press, since the coffee has more contact with the water and can steep evenly. Burr grinders are more technical, and have more adjustability when grinding coffee. Most coffee shops use burr grinders to prepare grounds for brewing, so you can be sure that these grinders will consistently give you good grounds no matter the brew method. Burr grinders work by having two pieces called burrs, either flat or conical, that are spaced out according to a grind setting

---

[1] See chapter 6, *How Should I Keep This Coffee From Going Bad?*, for a more detailed explanation on keeping coffee fresher for longer.

on the machine. Typically, the lower the number, the finer the grind, and the smaller the particles will be. While they are more expensive than blade grinders, they do produce more consistent particle sizes through the grind and will be more consistent over time.

In addition to a good grinder and brewing device, having a timer and scale will help you to produce a high quality cup of coffee time after time. Measuring out the coffee (and water, if you're using a hand brew technique) to ensure that you're putting the exact amount needed into your filter is good practice to reduce waste and make your bag of beans last longer. A standard ratio to use when figuring out how much coffee to use is one part coffee to 16 parts water. When purchasing a scale, I recommend looking for one that has a metric function to display grams, since the metric system is more precise than American measurements (sorry, America), and make sure the scale has a capacity of at least 2000g with 0.1g precision (listed as 2000g x 0.1g). In conjunction with having a scale, if you're using a hand brewing method over an automatic brewer, having a timer will help you to measure out both the length of your brew time as well as assign pouring weights to different times. This also is a way to standardize brewing so you can replicate your coffee making every time you want to make a cup yourself.

The final piece of equipment I recommend is a gooseneck kettle. For those of you, like me, who like to make coffee by hand, a gooseneck kettle is a must-buy. Unlike a standard tea kettle, which has a spout that pours out water at fairly fast rate and offers little control, a gooseneck kettle allows you to restrict the flow rate of the water to either extend or shorten your pour time as needed. You have a wide range of control, which is optimal for hand brewing methods like Chemex, V60, Kalita Wave, and Aeropress.

Choosing Your Method

Moving forward with all the tools needed to make your coffee, the next step is to choose how you want to make your cup. Do you want a way to fully immerse yourself in the coffee experience, or are you really in the mood for some quick caffeine? Do you want to do the work, or let the machines work for you? How much coffee are you wanting to drink? Do you want something hot or iced? Much like going to a coffee shop, the questions involved with your at home brewing methods are important to consider before you start the process. Each question goes hand in hand with each other, and can be asked in no particular order.

Sit And Stay Vs. On The Go

Coffee making and drinking, as mentioned earlier, can be a therapeutic experience. It can be as long or as short as you prefer, depending on the way your days look. The first major question you have to consider before you fire up the water kettle is: do I want to sit and sip on this coffee, or am I in a hurry? Different hand brew methods can take different lengths of time; most Aeropress recipes take less than two minutes start to finish, while some Kalita Wave recipes can take up to five minutes of pouring alone, not including the drawdown times. If you opt for an automatic brewing option, then your time decreases, which helps when you're on the go.

Auto Vs. Hand Brew

Speaking of choosing between automatic and hand brewing, with the innovation of brewing methods in both realms, the choice really comes down to your level of comfort: do you want to press a button and let the machine do the work, or do you want to have control of every variable in the brewing process? In the automatic brewing line up, manufacturers like Bonavita and Technivorm have had a corner on the market for years, with Technivorm's Moccamaster being the original specialty coffee auto brewer of choice. But, appliance companies like Cuisinart have been working hard to develop great machines, receiving certification by the Specialty Coffee Association (SCA) for two of their creations. In the hand brewing line up, you really get to pick your poison. Chemex has been around since the 1940's and shows no signs of going away anytime soon. And it seems like new companies are producing brewing methods everyday.

What's important to note about the difference between manual versus automatic brewing is the level of control involved. Technology within automatic brewing has advanced so far within the past decade that users can adjust parameters for dispersing water down to the second and gram. You can replicate brewing recipes with precision with each and every cup, which takes the worry out of coffee making. But, one down side of automatic brewers is that they can't account for anomalies in independent variables such as grind size and dry weight of coffee; it can't intelligently increase the amount of agitation to move the grounds around in the filter if a grind size is too coarse, or reduce agitation if the grind size is too fine. On the flip side, manual brewing gives you complete control of every extraction variable[2] on demand. You can account for any anomalies that may occur. But, you

---

[2] The main variables of extraction are: brew/dwell time, water temperature, turbulence/agitation, grind size, water quality, brewing method, and brewing ratio.

also control water flow rate, brew time, agitation, and extraction rate, which can make or break your cup of coffee if you don't have a recipe to reference or a good understanding of how your equipment works.

One Cup Vs. Multiple Cups

Figuring out how much coffee you want to consume in a sitting is pretty vital as well, since that influences your brewing ratio and, in some points, your brewing method. Mr. Coffee-style coffee makers can make up to eight cups in one serving, which is great for the office dweller who needs to keep focused on his work and needs to stay awake with multiple cups of coffee. French presses make two to three cups normally, and are helpful for those who want to have a hand in their brew method, but don't want to step fully into controlling too much at once. Conical hand brew methods, like Chemexes and V60's, can make around one to two cups, and is great for the home brewer who enjoys the science and art behind brewing.

Hot Vs. Cold

The temperature of your coffee makes a difference in how you brew as well. Since most drinks are enjoyable either piping hot or ice cold, choosing whether you want hot or iced coffee is pretty much the only temperature decision you have to make. Methods like immersion and drip cold brewers, while they take time, create great iced coffee options that bring out flavor while highlighting the full body of the method. Iced coffee is great for a hot day where you want to keep cool, but still caffeinate like normal.

Variables Of Brewing

While brewing a cup of coffee isn't rocket science, it still is a scientific equation that contains independent variables, dependent variables, constants, and controls. It's not as complicated as high school chemistry, but the equation does merit some consideration. What you're seeking to do in brewing coffee is extract all the "good stuff" contained within your beans, also known as the soluble content, using hot water, also known as the solute. In this equation, you have seven main variables to consider.

How you control these variables will also control the strength of your coffee. While some refer to strength in regards to roast level, like we mentioned in the second chapter, strength really correlates with extraction; higher extraction rates (more of the good stuff) produce a perceived stronger cup of coffee, while lower extraction rates (less of the good stuff) produce a perceived weaker cup of coffee.

Brew/Dwell Time

Brew time and dwell time are two different parts of your recipe. Brew time refers to how long you're pouring your water, and dwell time refers to how long water is coming into contact with your grounds from start to finish. The longer the dwell time, the more the water extracts from the coffee.

Water Temperature

Not many people consider temperature as an important part of brewing, but it's vital to maintaining the other variables. Keeping temperature between 198° and 202° F is the optimal temperature for pulling out soluble content.

Turbulence/Agitation

Agitation refers to the rate at which water unsettles and stirs up the coffee grounds. A lighter flow rater creates light agitation, which leaves the coffee grounds tighter in place, while a heavier flow rate creates heavy agitation, which moves around the grounds and allows water to pull out more from the coffee.

Grind Size

Grind size either decreases the density of coffee particles with a finer grind size, or increases it with a coarser grind size. Adjusting grind size will adjust the surface area of the coffee grounds, allowing quicker or slower water absorption and dispersion back into the water.

Water Quality

Believe it or not, how refined your water is matters concerning how your coffee will taste. If the chemicals in your tap water (yes, there are chemicals in there from the treatment plant) aren't well balanced, ultimately what's in the water will react with the coffee differently than water with well balanced chemistry. Products like Third Wave Water will provide the most optimal minerals to distilled water in order to bring out the best taste from your coffee.

Brewing Method

The kind of brewer you use will promote different extraction rates and ultimately reveal different nuances of the coffee. Immersion methods will increase body, while filter methods will enhance clarity. Conical filter methods provide a smaller margin for error and compensates for any anomalies, since all the water flows through the tip of the filter, while flat bottom filter methods have a wider margin for error, since water travels through a smaller portion of coffee.

Brewing Ratio

How much water and how much coffee you use will influence how readily coffee will extract. If you use too much coffee, your coffee will taste bitter and muddy due to over-extraction. If you use too little coffee, your coffee will taste acidic and too light due to under-extraction. The same concept applies to water; too much water means your coffee will be over-extracted, and too little water means your coffee will be under-extracted.

Brewing Guides

This is where the rubber meets the road. You have your coffee, and now you get to have fun. Looking back on the tools you need readily available[3], all you have to do is brew. Each of the brew methods listed can be found on sites like Amazon and are relatively inexpensive. Keep in mind the variables that will ultimately affect extraction, and remember that you are in control. Following these guides will help you brew like a pro, and experience a great cup of coffee time after time. Be as intentional as you can with hitting targets, but don't beat yourself up if you pour an extra 10g or accidentally pour too fast. The guides will reflect grind settings on a Baratza Encore, a 40-setting grinder, and will yield roughly 12oz of coffee.

Each brew method works best when you pre-wet the filters with at-temperature water. Pre-wetting the filter both heats up the brew method, keeps the brewed coffee from absorbing into the filter, and eliminates the papery taste that comes from the filter itself.

---

[3] See pp. 54-57.

Chemex

Developed in the 1940's, Chemex has been a staple in home brewing. With the brewer and decanter all in one, it's a space-saving tool that produces a solid cup of coffee.

- Heat 420g water to 205° F
- Weigh out 25g coffee, and grind at 22-25 on the Encore (medium-coarse grind size)
- Pour 30-50g water slowly onto the grounds, then start timer
- At 0:30, begin pouring mildly heavily to 300g, which should occur at 1:00, then stop pouring
- From 1:00 to 1:30, let the slurry draw down
- At 1:30, being pouring to 400g, which should occur at 1:45, then stop pouring
- The slurry should draw down and stop dripping between 3:20 and 3:45

Expect a balanced body, clear taste notes, and pleasant acidity.

V60

A Swiss Army Knife in the brewing world, the V60 is a great option to create a fully balanced cup of coffee. The conical shape of the brewer helps encourage water contact with the grounds, allowing for proper extraction throughout.

- Heat 420g water to 205° F
- Weigh out 25g coffee, and grind at 17-20 on the Encore (medium grind size)
- Pour 30-50g water slowly onto the grounds, then start timer
- At 0:30, begin pouring, washing the walls of the filter to saturate the outlying grounds, then bring your water stream back to the center of the slurry, pouring nickel-sized circles
- At 1:00/200g, make three filter-washing passes, then return to the nickel-sized circles
- At 1:15/300g, make three filter-washing passes, then return to the nickel-sized circles
- At 1:30/400g, finish your pour
- The slurry should draw down between 2:20 and 2:45

Expect a symmetrically balanced cup: mild body, equal presentation of notes, and slight yet approachable acidity.

Iced V60

Following the standard V60 recipe is the iced version. If you want to enjoy a hand brewed coffee but over ice, this is the choice for you. The brightness and clarity of the coffee shines through even at a lower temperature. This pulse recipe adds 60g of water with every segment, and uses half the water but the same dry dose.

- Heat 235g water to 205° F
- Weigh out 25g coffee, and grind at 17-20 on the Encore (medium grind size)
- Pour 30-50g water slowly onto the grounds, then start timer
- At 0:30, begin pouring, washing the walls of the filter to saturate the outlying grounds, pouring in a spiral pattern
- At 0:45/100g, stop pouring
- At 0:55, begin pouring again in a spiral pattern
- At 1:10/160g, stop pouring
- At 1:15, begin pouring again in a spiral pattern
- At 1:30/215g, finish your pour
- The slurry should draw down between 2:20 and 2:45

Expect a crisp, refreshing cup of flash-brewed coffee that highlights sweetness and presents slight acidity.

Gino/Kalita Wave

Flat bottom drippers like Gino and Kalita Wave bring out body more readily, helping you to produce a "stronger" cup of coffee and avoiding the bitterness that over-extraction highlights. While this is a more time-consuming method, it's great for days when you have a few extra minutes to spare.

- Heat 420g water to 205° F
- Weigh out 25g coffee, and grind at 22-25 on the Encore (medium-coarse grind size)
- Pour 30-50g water slowly onto the grounds, then start timer
- At 0:30, begin pouring, washing the walls of the filter to saturate the outlying grounds, pouring in a continuous spiral pattern throughout the brewing method
- At 1:00, aim to be at 100g
- At 1:20, aim to be at 200g
- At 1:40, aim to be at 300g
- At 2:00, finish pouring
- The slurry should draw down between 3:15 and 3:30

Expect a full body, heavier mouthfeel, and refined sweetness as the cup cools.

Aeropress

A modern brewing method, the Aeropress is a multi-use tool that travels well and has a narrow margin for error. You can either eyeball your measurements due to the numbers on the side, or be precise through using a scale.

- Heat 300g water to 205° F
- Weigh out 15g coffee, and grind at 17-20 on the Encore (medium grind size)
- Place Aeropress on decanter/mug, filter basket down
- Pour 60g (or to the "1"), then start timer
- Stir 10 times after starting the timer
- At 0:30, pour to 250g (or to the "4")
- Insert plunger at an angle, then slightly pull up to create vacuum
- At 1:45, begin pushing plunger
- The brewer should begin hissing at 2:10, and pushing should be complete at 2:15

Expect to clean yet smaller cup of coffee that especially brings out citrus and fruit notes that may be present.

French Press

One of the most recognizable brewing methods outside of a Mr. Coffee, the french press makes a full body cup of coffee that will make even the least experienced coffee drinker happy. There's very little margin for error, which makes it a simple method to use. Having a spoon handy for this method is recommended.

- Heat 420g of water to 205° F
- Weigh out 30g coffee, and grind at 26-30 on the Encore (coarse grind)
- Simultaneously start timer while beginning the pour, and pour 400g all at once, aiming to finish pour at 0:30
- Once finished pouring, stir grounds and water for 15 seconds
- Place plunger top, keeping plunger at top of the glass
- At 4:00, press plunger and serve

Expect one to two cups of coffee that has a heavy mouthfeel, chocolatey notes, and all around a crowd pleaser.

Brewing coffee is a fun activity that, when applying these concepts properly, will yield a delicious cup every single time you step up to the kitchen counter and pull out the tools you need. You need not be intimidated by the variables of brewing, but rather appreciate them for what they're worth; they help you to figure out what influences your extraction and inform you on how to control each part of the equation.

Part Three: How To Drink Later

How Should I Keep This Coffee From Going Bad?

What a relief it is to have a freshly brewed cup of coffee in the comfort of your own home. In the long run, if you drink only brewed coffee, you end up saving more money than going to a coffee shop even three days a week. But, now you're faced with a decision: how can I keep this coffee fresher for longer? What's the best way to get the best use out of my purchase? Ultimately, for how long is this coffee drinkable? Most bags of coffee within the specialty coffee industry comes with a single date: the date on which the coffee was roasted. What does that mean for me at home? Keeping coffee fresh and usable has long been a marginalized topic, and when brought up, most professionals will act nonchalantly about the answer; somehow we should all know best practice when it comes to our retail coffee.

The unfortunate truth is that coffee gets old. The compounds break down, dulling taste as time marches on. But, there is a window in which coffee is best used and consumed. Referring back to the roast date, the date listed indicates day one of the coffee's lifespan. Between days one and three of the coffee's life, the beans will be producing a large amounts of gas that give it its fragrance, but also hinder proper extraction; when you brew a pour-over of a coffee that is less than three days off roast, you'll experience a large amount of bubbling in your slurry. That bubbling is gases being released as the grounds make contact with water, and too much gas present is a sign that the coffee needed to rest longer and that your coffee isn't going through proper extraction. After three to four days, the gas production in the beans stabilizes, allowing for replicable and repeatable brewing over the next three weeks. Typically, the taste notes listed on the packaging come through clean and clear when the coffee is properly extracted. After 14 to 21 days, the coffee begins to taste dull as gas production has slowed. You'll tend to see less bubbling in the slurry, which is a tell-tale sign that your coffee is losing freshness.

Some roasters will also include a second date stamp: a "use by" or "sell by" date. There's a difference between the roast date and the "sell by" date, which is important to note when comparing coffees. Most regulatory agencies, especially those that approve products going into the grocery and retail stores, will require roasters to include a date relating to the suggested end of its shelf life. While coffee does have a shelf life of up to six months, the shelf life is well past the universally recommended period of use. The "sell by" date may also indicate a lesser quality of coffee; displaying an elongated shelf life for something that changes over time is a red flag that a preservative might have been added in the roasting process[1]. So, do your best to evaluate your choices based on the roast date instead of any other listed dates.

The Enemies Of Coffee

If you take an overview of coffee packaging across the spectrum, you'll notice a few different types of bags/containers: tin or plastic cans with lids, foil-lined bags that roll down with posable tabs, zipper bags, bags with one way valves, bags with no valve, etc. Some companies prefer a packaging method that might be in line with their brand, while other value functionality and efficiency. All of these packages are trying to achieve the same goal: to keep out air, water, and light. These three environmental factors are ultimately the enemies of coffee at some point in its roasted lifespan.

Prolonged exposure to the air will ultimately bring about a staling effect to coffee. Air ends up encouraging the aromatic compounds

---

[1] A major exception to this is Intelligentsia Coffee, who retail their bags nationwide and have high quality beans throughout all of their offerings.

that give coffee its dry fragrance to release and escape too soon. When the aromatic compounds are gone, there is very little within the brewing process that can coax out those prominent flavors that distinguish that coffee from another. Any exposure to water, whether whole bean or ground, will cause the extraction process to begin within coffee. Moisture introduced prematurely in coffee's lifespan will spoil the coffee for when you prepare to brew it, and could create an over-extracted cup with slightly moldy taste notes. Steady light exposure, especially in an enclosed and/or clear container, will also encourage aromatics to release from the beans. With air, water, and light present at any point in your coffee prior to brewing, it could very well end up being a recipe for disaster.

Storing Coffee

In order to avoid these three environmental factors, a few different options are available for your consideration. Not everyone has the space, access, and ability to keep their coffee in the darkest, driest, and closest to airtight place, especially if you live in a small apartment or in a fairly humid area. But ultimately, you can control how much exposure no matter what your situation is. These basic storage tips are achievable with ease.

Now, before proceeding with these tips, if you have the ability to purchase a bag of whole bean coffee from a roaster that uses a one-way valve, has a zipper closure, and is completely opaque, then I would consider it wise to look at their offerings first. Not every roaster packages coffee with these three components present, so be aware of that as you buy your beans next time. If you find a bag of coffee that you really like, but one of these options is missing, this is where these storage tips come into handy.

Whole Bean Vs. Pre-Ground

It would be naïve of me to assume that everyone reading this can afford a grinder to grind beans on demand. For the longest time, I personally didn't even have a grinder at my disposal, and shied away from even purchasing coffee beans to take home as a result. So, it would seem to be the most convenient choice present for someone who doesn't have a grinder to be to buy pre-ground coffee. But, I would suggest, even urge, that you do whatever you can not to buy pre-ground coffee.

Roasted coffee naturally produces gases at a regular rate; it's unavoidable and part of the aging process. That's the source of the fragrance you get when you take a big whiff from the one-way valve on some bags. When roasted coffee stays in whole bean form, the gases release at a slower rate than when ground. The aromatic compounds at work within the coffee help preserve the flavor, aroma, and overall resiliency of the beans.

Having a coffee shop grind your retail coffee before you leave can be helpful if you plan on using that coffee shortly after purchasing it, i.e., within a week or two. But, once you get past the first 10 days, quality starts to deteriorate and the coffee becomes stale. So, if at all possible, do whatever you can to keep from grinding beans prior to brewing. If that means purchasing a cheap blade grinder from Wal-Mart, then so be it. But, you will not regret having your coffee stay fresher for longer.

In Bag Vs. In A Canister

Packaging itself can prove to be a frustration; sometimes too much air gets trapped in the bag when you seal it, sometimes the can doesn't seal properly, and sometimes the posable flaps on the bag don't fold like they're supposed to. It's a headache when making sure that your coffee stays untouched by the elements. But, does it warrant buying a completely different container to store beans?

There are a few things to think about: space, regularity of use, material, and durability. If you don't have the cabinet space to store a coffee canister, or if the canisters available can't fit the coffee you've bought, then it isn't smart to buy one. If you're opening up the canister multiple times a day and there isn't an air release port, then it probably would be best to stick with the bag. But, if you open the canister maybe once a day or every other day, then it might be a good option. If the canister is made of a low-grade plastic that might be better suited for storing baking materials like flour or sugar, then maybe use it for that instead. But, if the canister is specifically tested for use with coffee, that would be a worthwhile option. And if the canister itself cannot withstand normal wear-and-tear from the inevitable drops, then it probably isn't worth your money.

On Counter Vs. In Cabinet

Often a topic of debate within the home barista world, where in your house you store your beans, whether in canister or in bag, is oddly important. Most wouldn't think this is as vital to coffee freshness as it is, but you'd be surprised. The big variable in the debate is light exposure: which location reduces the most amount of contact with natural light? The location where you store your beans mildly depends on the container you're using; most roasters have opaque bags for their packaging, so if you keep your beans in the bag in which you purchased them, you should be just fine to keep them on your counter by your brewing setup, or on a shelf to display your spoils to all who enter your home. But, if you have a clear or translucent canister, or a canister made of tin or some kind of metal, it's best to store your beans in a cabinet away from light exposure. With little to no way for the heat energy created by direct light exposure to escape through these canisters, on-counter storage expedites the aging process significantly in comparison with in-cabinet storage.

Freezing

A relatively newer option to the storage conversation, freezing coffee is actually a good alternative for those who may not go through beans that quickly. While it has its warnings and precautions, putting coffee beans in a sealed, freezer-burn-proof bag slows the aging process significantly, eliminating air and light exposure and essentially causing the compounds within the beans to go dormant. I've seen beans that are months old, when properly defrosted and prepared for brewing, taste like they're within the first few days off-roast. It's a method that could revolutionize your brewing, if you're a casual, occasional brewer.

But, freezing coffee comes with its warnings. With the main freezing agent within a kitchen freezer being water, you run the risk of contaminating your beans if you don't store them in the right packaging, just like you would with meats and freezer burn. If you choose to freeze your coffee, be sure to place the original packaging inside a gallon freezer bag that will protect your coffee from water exposure. When you take your coffee out to brew again, take into consideration that, just like with meat, you have to bring the beans to a regulated temperature; you can't just throw frozen beans into your grinder and brew like nothing happened. During the thawing process, monitor the moisture content that will inevitably come as a result. You can take a paper towel and dab any water that you see forming in order to absorb it and eliminate extra exposure. Once the beans get to room temperature and no longer have a cool feel to the touch, then your beans will be ready to brew. This process may take 15 to 20 minutes, if not longer, so be prepared to account for this time increase.

While coffee has a window freshness, taking extra steps to eliminate factors that might seek to narrow that timeframe is essential in brewing coffee at home. Different storage methods are readily available, and usually affordably priced in your local Target or Wal-Mart. If you live a fast paced life and have less time than you would like to brew coffee daily, don't let your high quality beans go to waste; take the time to preserve your beans, and don't fret if all you can do is keep your bag on the counter. Keeping your beans fresh is all about continuing your brewing journey, and part of that journey is figuring out what works best for you.

Epilogue

Everything that you've just read will help you make better use of your coffee, but it's simply a foundation. From the origins of coffee to brewing it for yourself, we've skimmed just the surface of what goes on with coffee. So much more exists within the coffee world, and you truly have the sky as your limit to knowledge. As you close this book, having the information needed to be dangerous in the café queue line and the confidence to make coffee at home, don't stop here. Keep reading. Ask questions of your local baristas about their coffees, what they do to grow in their craft, and how to get ahold of the resources for yourself. Use websites like Daily Coffee News and Sprudge to read "insider information" on the way that coffee is growing across America and across the world.

More than anything, don't just take what you hear at face value within the coffee realm. Check and double check the ideas, thoughts, and news that you may hear in passing or read as you scroll through the headlines. Be an informed coffee drinker, and do your part to contribute to the growth of specialty coffee, and coffee in general, in your area.

Without you, reader, our industry is nothing. Whether you're a seasoned veteran barista who's paid his or her dues over the years, a regular customer at the shop down the street from your house, or a grocery-store coffee buyer: you matter to the growth of our work and efforts. Thank you for your patronage, thank you for reading this book, and thank you for going out from here to make the world a more caffeinated place.

As always, happy brewing.

For more information, updates, and all things coffee related, be sure to follow @coffeforeverydayuse, both on Instagram and Facebook

About The Author

Jacob Ray is a coffee professional based out of Nashville, Tennessee. Working in shops all around the coffee-enriched city, he has been able to see how different concepts, processes, and overall practice is best conducted. Serving in roles from barista, shift leader, and store manager, all the way up to director of roasting, wholesale director, quality and education director, and green buyer, he has a wide array of experience within the industry.

When he's not at work or making coffee, Jacob is with his beautiful wife, Alley, and their dog, Tod. The two enjoy hiking, going on road trips, and overall travels that include seeing more of the beautiful parts that make up America.

Prior to coffee, Jacob worked in ministry for six years, teaching students and heading up creative departments across the Southeast. He believes that coffee is now his ministry, engaging people from all walks of life to think differently with each sip.

Made in the USA
Columbia, SC
03 February 2020

87229120R00059